AESCHYLUS

The Suppliants

THE LOCKERT LIBRARY

OF POETRY IN TRANSLATION

A complete list of titles
in the Lockert Library appears
on page 61

AESCHYLUS
The Suppliants

TRANSLATED BY

PETER BURIAN

PRINCETON UNIVERSITY PRESS

Published by Princeton University Press, 41 William Street,
Princeton, New Jersey 08540
In the United Kingdom: Princeton University Press, Oxford

Library of Congress Cataloging-in-Publication Data

Aeschylus.
[Suppliants. English]
The suppliants / Aeschylus ; translated by Peter Burian.
p.   cm.—(Lockert library of poetry in translation)
Includes bibliographical references.
ISBN 0-691-06867-4 — ISBN 0-691-01495-7
1. Danaus (Legendary character)—Drama. I. Burian, Peter, 1943–
II. Title. III. Series.
PA3827.S7B87 1991   008'.01—dc20   90-9007

The Lockert Library of Poetry in Translation is supported by a bequest from
Charles Lacy Lockert (1888–1974)

This book has been composed in Linotron Bembo

Princeton University Press books are printed on acid-free paper, and meet the
guidelines for permanence and durability of the Committee on Production
Guidelines for Book Longevity of the Council on Library Resources

Printed in the United States of America by Princeton University Press,
Princeton, New Jersey

1 3 5 7 9 10 8 6 4 2

1 3 5 7 9 10 8 6 4 2

(pbk.)

Designed by Laury A. Egan

For Maura

ἐρᾷ μὲν ἁγνὸς οὐρανὸς τρῶσαι χθόνα,
ἔρως δέ γαῖαν λαμβάνει γάμου τυχεῖν,
ὄμβρος δ᾽ ἀπ᾽ εὐνάοντος οὐρανοῦ πεσὼν
ἔκυσε γαῖαν· ἡ δὲ τίκτεται βροτοῖς
μήλων τε βοσκὰς καὶ βίον Δημήτριον·
δενδρῶτις ὥρα δ᾽ ἐκ νοτίζοντος γάμου
τέλειός ἐστι. τῶνδ᾽ ἐγὼ παραίτιος.

CONTENTS

ACKNOWLEDGMENTS

This translation began more than twenty years ago, with the excuse of a stalled dissertation and the encouragement of two mentors and friends, W. Robert Connor and the late Robert D. Murray, Jr. Bob Murray was kind enough to give me a copy of his own unpublished version and to discuss a number of difficult passages with me at length. Alas, it is no longer possible to know what he would think of the result, but his love of the *Suppliants*, and the deep understanding of its workings embodied in his book on *The Motif of Io in Aeschylus' "Suppliants"* (Princeton 1958), were essential to me as I set out on the long path that has led me here. Many friends have helped along the way; I want to mention a salutary critique by William Arrowsmith at an early (and very unsatisfactory) stage, and the sympathetic readings of later drafts by James Applewhite, Haun Saussy, Gordon Campbell, Sharon Ryan, and William C. Scott. I owe most of all to the encouragement and the editorial skill of Maura High. I am grateful also to the students who have had this obsession of mine foisted upon them and have responded with tolerance and even (or so it seemed) pleasure.

INTRODUCTION

On Translating the *Suppliants*

Aeschylus' *Suppliants* has long since passed from the hands of educated generalists to those of the specialist. Whatever reputation it had was due to the long-standing belief that its preponderance of choral lyric made it the earliest extant tragedy, an archaic work of not much later than 490 B.C. That theory was exploded in the 1950s by the publication of a scrap of Egyptian papyrus that almost certainly assigns *Suppliants* to the mid-460s. Take away primacy of date, and what is left is a Greek tragedy that resolutely refuses to include most of the elements we expect of Greek tragedy: no hero, no *hamartia*, no downfall or tragic conclusion of any kind. The myth itself is obscure and Aeschylus' treatment of it largely open to conjecture, since the play we have is only the first in a connected tetralogy whose other parts have disappeared almost without trace. Even the text of this orphan is unusually corrupt and fraught with uncertainties; the experts agree in calling *Suppliants* the most difficult of Aeschylus' plays to interpret.

What is in it, then, for the translator, and what for that educated generalist whom the translator must be hoping against hope to reach? For one thing, a succession of choral odes that are among the densest, most opulent, most purely lovely things in all Greek poetry. For another, a world at once remote and exotic, yet primal in its evocation of the struggle of male and female, its enactment of terror, cunning, and lust, its insistence on the presence of the sacred in the world. And not least, though perhaps most surprising, a skeletal but gripping drama of civic crisis, of ideologies in conflict and clashing forms of power.

The question, "Why translate?" is not the same for a work that has never appeared in our language as for one like *Suppliants* that has been Englished, in verse and prose, scores of times over several centuries. Love of the text, even fresh critical insights into it, do not in themselves authorize yet another version. I began, as I imagine most retranslators do, out of dissatisfaction with earlier attempts. The translations I knew seemed on the whole to be pedestrian pieces of writing, sometimes oddly cavalier in their rendering of the Greek, and certainly not mirrors of the musical splendor I had begun to hear in Aeschylus' verse, nor of the concentrated power of his diction. My initial efforts forced me to reassess the standard by which I had been presuming to judge. But it was a new translation of *Suppliants*, one of an altogether higher order of ambition and accomplishment, that paradoxically spurred me to try again and showed me how. This was Janet Lembke's version, which appeared in 1975 in William Arrowsmith's Oxford series of Greek Tragedy in New Translations.

In Lembke I found a translator who took Aeschylus' verbal magic seriously and searched seriously for emotional equivalents in our own idiom. At its most effective, her version brilliantly reappropriates and bodies forth the ancient sense of awe still so strong in Aeschylus:

> on earth a godhost gives
>   order to nature
>   Which god shall I cry to?
>   Whose acts will answer me?
> The Father
>   Urge of my green life
>   Whose own hand has sown me

Lord
      Ancient in wisdom Who crafted my people
      Allhelp
      Whose fair breath has sped me
Zeus

In high fiery places He sits
      suppliant to no throne
            nor derives His might
            from a more potent king
No other
      enforces His homage
      nor is He valley overshadowed by summits
But He
      acts in the instant of speech
      His word
      has completed whatever His will
conceives

O Father Lord Zeus no other but He conceives Father

Here was something of the raw force and depth of feeling that makes reading Aeschylus so exhilarating. But it also appeared to me that Lembke had purchased that not inconsiderable virtue at the price of downplaying the formal magnificence, the compact intricacy of Aeschylean verse. And in their place, she seemed to feel the need to heighten and glamorize his images ("urge of my green life" and "nor is He valley overshadowed by summits" are in effect kennings only indirectly related to the Greek text, and the first and final lines are more or less free invention). There seemed still to be room for a version that reflected more fully what is classical in the art of Aeschylus: strong emotion compressed to the bursting point by the rigor of formal constraint.

    The essential formal feature of choral lyric, such as the passage we have been examining (lines 590–99 in the Greek, 790–815 in Lembke, 582–97 in the present version) is *strophic re-*

sponsion, that is, the articulation of the ode in pairs of metrically matched stanzas. It occurred to me that I could at once stay closer to the Greek and give the requisite discipline to my verse by strict syllabic responsion, a device that declares (without attempting to reproduce) the difference between Greek and English versification, but still gives a strong sense of form:

> What god have I clearer
> claim in justice
> to summon for his deeds
> than the Father
> who planted my seed with his own hand,
> great architect of our race,
> allhealer, old in wisdom,
> Zeus of fair breezes?
>
> He sits below the throne
> of no other,
> to no power pays homage,
> does no one's work
> but his own. His deeds are accomplished
> with the whisper of a word
> that brings to birth whatever
> his fertile mind wills.

A second formal decision, in my mind really a corollary of the first, was to emphasize the difference between choral lyric (sung, danced) and the spoken dialogue that dominates the episodes. (Indeed, one standard formal element within episodes, called *kommos*, is an exchange between chorus and actor in which different degrees of emotional engagement and rational control are indicated by having one party sing and the other respond in spoken verse.) This bursting from speech into song is perhaps the single most striking stylistic feature of Greek tragedy, and the one least clear in most current translations. I have attempted to represent it by using relaxed blank verse for spoken dialogue to contrast with the lyric syllabics. Needless to say, reporting such decisions as these gives no idea of the process of translating, with its alternations of exhilarating discovery and deeply frustrating feelings of inadequacy. One has the sensation of coming closer to the poem than anyone but its first maker, and at the same time one cannot escape the recognition that one's best efforts are bound to fall short of what he made. Apart from the sheer beauty of the verse—that constant *croce e delizia*, spur and reproach—the most daunting element of *Suppliants* proved, for me at least, to be the prodigious thematic density of the text. Even in the simplest narrative contexts, I found myself constantly risking what might seem to be overtranslation in order to do some kind of justice to the elaborate verbal connections latent in apparently innocent expressions.

Here is an example, from a passage of dialogue that is quite straightforward in its denotation and not highly wrought in the way that many of the lyrics certainly are. Danaos, the father of the Suppliants, is recounting events that took place (offstage) in the Argive assembly:

> King Pelasgos
> won our case with a warning not to fatten
> the wrath of Zeus Lord of Suppliants.
> Twofold defilement, he said, arising alike
> from claims of natives and strangers, would wander the
> state,
> grazing unchecked, insatiable for suffering.
> The people of Argos heard and stretched their hands
> high even before the vote was called.
> Skillful turns of speech persuaded them,
> but Zeus put his seal on the outcome, too.
> (ll. 611–20)

I have taken a hint from the vivid *pachunai*, "fatten" (an image Aeschylus liked in this kind of context; there is, for example, a memorable evocation of the blood-sated Fury of the House of Atreus as the "thrice-fattened [*tripachunton*] spirit of the race" in his *Agamemnon*) and the rather neutral *boskema*, in this context "food," to produce a picture of a quasi-personified defilement that roams Argos like a herd of famished cattle. But this is hardly overtranslating, it seems to me, because it picks up Io the ancestral cow, Epaphos the calf of Zeus, and the subsidiary motifs of herds, grazing, and the like, given such prominence throughout the play. *Boskema*, though apparently unrelated etymologically to *bous*, the word for cow that is used alone or in compounds some twenty times in the play, is one of a number of words that are closely associated by sound and meaning with cattle imagery. In other contexts, indeed, it denotes "that which is fed," i.e., in the first instance, cattle. But, if we allow the presence of cows in this passage, we must also recognize that Aeschylus is not merely reinforcing a dominant image, but making it richly equivocal. For cattle are now not merely associated with the sufferings of the suppliants and their much-tried foremother Io, but also with the suffering that they themselves threaten. This kind of thematic density serves to introduce central tensions and contradictions.

But these few, simple lines contain at least two other significant thematic "equivocators." The choice of "grazing" for *boskema* made it impossible for me to bring out a connection of some significance between its modifier *amechanon*, here "without remedy, irresistible," and the *mechane*, "device" (453, 456), that the Danaids desperately threaten—hanging themselves from the images of the gods, the horrible defilement that wins their acceptance by King Pelasgos in the first place. Again, there is a significant verbal nexus, only part of which I found it possible to make overt. "Turn plan into deed," Danaos tells his daughters (205), urging them to take their places at the altars of the gods: *mechanes d' esto kratos*, literally, "let there be command of the device." "I am at wit's end," says Pelasgos (365), using the verbal form *amechano*, as he confronts the political crisis thrust upon him by the Danaids' supplication. At the end of the play, the Danaids leave to take refuge behind "towers designed / with deep cunning" (976–77), *purgon batheiai mechanei*, literally, "a deep device of towers." And in the final words of the play, they pray for "some cunning device to win my deliverance."

Lastly, the final phrase of this speech, "but Zeus put his seal on the outcome, too," involves one of *Suppliants'* most richly ambiguous terms, *telos* (variously "end," "goal," "fulfillment," "power," and more; it occurs along with its cognates no fewer than nineteen times in this play). The *telos* that the Danaids seek is escape from a marriage they do not want, but the word itself and its compounds are often used precisely in reference to marriage, as the normal goal or outcome of maturation (thus, at 1049, "marriage rites" renders the phrase *telos . . . Kutherieas*, "goal of the love goddess"). The Danaids pray to Zeus for deliverance, as the most powerful of gods: "yours is the power / in perfect fulfillment" (514–15: *teleon teleiotaton kratos*), but above all as their ancestor, the lover who ended the sufferings of their foremother Io by the fertile touch and breath that engendered her child. Thus his power, his *telos*, works ironically against the Danaids' wishes, and the phrase in question here, *Zeus d' epekranen telos* (literally, "and Zeus ratified the result"), cannot help but be shadowed by the figure of Zeus the Fulfiller setting his seal on very different outcomes—the acceptance of sexuality, the blessing of offspring, and the founding of a great line.

I hope that this elaborate discussion of a simple passage will serve to suggest some of the thought processes that go into making the vast number of choices out of which the verbal fabric of a translation is made, the kinds of local victories and defeats that mark the process of translating. But of course choice and interpretative cunning can only domesticate the beast to a certain point. If at times the language and "feel" of this version seem odd, this reflects something that one perhaps comes to understand more intimately as a translator of ancient Greek than as a scholar, the deep unfamiliarity, the strangeness of the culture and its poetic imagination. Especially with a text as difficult and often doubtful as *Suppliants*, scholarly caution must simply yield to a poetic leap of faith, and the process becomes an act of appropriating and re-creating that is only partly conscious. Still, a translator who is also a scholar will be acutely aware that the result is like an image captured in a distorting mirror. That, in turn, suggests why the major monuments of past literatures can and indeed must be translated again and again: each image will be distorted in a different way, refracted by the atmosphere of its own place and time. Each generation feels the need to hold up its own mirrors, not so much in the vain hope of finding one that will reflect with perfect accuracy as in search of one whose images, at least for the moment, seem to flicker with life.

The dominant view of translation in our literary tradition—shaped perhaps by tensions connected with translating the biblical Word—is as a parasitic, or even parricidal, activity, a necessary betrayal, a well-meaning threat to the truth of the text. Translators who feel that their job is already hard enough will more readily accept the idea, developed in our time with great subtlety by Walter Benjamin and Jacques Derrida, that translating is a form of *writing*, not designed to reproduce, much less replace, an existing text, but to complement it and extend its life. Not Oedipal struggle, then, but a process of renewal and growth for works that would otherwise have only a vestigial existence, and, in the very greatest versions, new life for language itself. To continue the biological metaphor, a work that may have lain dormant for generations can suddenly send up new shoots and flourish in alien soil. All but a very few blossoms soon die back, but for the time of their blooming they make palpable the life in the roots. That is my wish for this version.

The Danaid Myth and Aeschylus' Tetralogy

The story upon which Aeschylus based his Danaid tetralogy is known to us from a variety of ancient sources, starting with

Hesiod and extending to the mythographers of late antiquity. It forms part of the legendary history of ancient Argos, in the Peloponnese, where *Suppliants* is set. The background given in the play itself varies only in details from the tale as it is told elsewhere. In remote times, when the rule of Zeus was still young, he made love to Io, a young Argive priestess of Hera. Hera, when she learned of the affair, transformed Io into a cow, but Zeus continued his visits in the form of a bull. Hera then set the hundred-eyed Argos on Io as a watchman, but he was killed by Hermes. Hera then sent a gadfly to sting Io into flight, and she crossed from Greece to Asia, then on to Egypt in her agony. But there, by the gentlest touch and breath, Zeus made her pregnant with the god Epaphos, who in turn fathered a glorious line that included, in the third generation, the brothers Danaos and Aigyptos. These two had, respectively, fifty daughters (the Danaids) and fifty sons (the Aigyptioi). The sons tried to force the daughters to marry them, but the Danaids fled to Argos with their father.

At this point our play begins. Its action is quickly told: the Danaids take refuge in a sanctuary shared by several gods outside the city, where the Argive king, Pelasgos comes to meet them. In an elaborate debate scene, they convince him to risk war by protecting them from the Aigyptioi, but only after they threaten to kill themselves at the altar, an act that would horribly pollute their place of refuge and bring the wrath of Zeus, protector of suppliants, upon the entire land. Pelasgos departs with Danaos to persuade the Argive people that they should grant the suppliants' plea, leaving the Danaids to pray for success; the old man returns to announce that the assembly has indeed given unanimous consent. At the conclusion of the Danaids' ode invoking blessings upon their new home, Danaos announces that he has seen the fleet of the Aigyptioi approaching harbor, and goes to summon help. The enemy herald enters with armed attendants and proceeds to cajole, threaten, and finally lay hands upon the Danaids, only to be stopped by the arrival of Pelasgos and his men. The herald withdraws after an acrimonious exchange, threatening war to come. Pelasgos invites the Danaids to enter the city, but they ask first for Danaos to return and advise them. Danaos urges modesty in the face of temptation in a strange city, and the concluding choral lyrics unexpectedly debate the wisdom of the Danaids' resolve to remain unwed.

Little survives of the remaining plays in Aeschylus' Danaid tetralogy, *Aigyptioi*, *Danaids*, and the satyr play *Amymone*. (Indeed, the possibility that *Aigyptioi* stood first in the group cannot be entirely eliminated.) From a number of sources, however, we have a pretty clear idea of the story they dramatized. In *Prometheus Bound*, a slightly later play of Aeschylus (or, as some classical scholars now believe, of an anonymous follower), the hero prophesies the arrival of the Danaids in Argos pursued by the sons of Aigyptos,

> who will come hunting marriages not to be hunted,
> but the god will begrudge them those bodies, and instead
> Pelasgos' land will receive them when they lie vanquished
> by women's bold blows in the watches of night.
> For his own wife will rob each husband of life,
> bathing her two-edged sword in blood: so may
> Love come to my enemies! But desire will beguile
> one girl to spare her bedmate, and she will blunt
> her intention, wishing rather to be called weak
> than a murderer. She will bear a race of kings
> in Argos. To make it clear needs a longer tale.
>
> (ll. 858–870)

There seems no reason to doubt that this is what *Aigyptioi* and *Danaids* were about, and other sources help us fill in details. (The story of Hypermestra, the Danaid who spares her bridegroom Lynkeus, is one of the most prominent features of almost every version of the myth, early and late.) The title *Aigyptioi* makes it highly probable that the sons of Aigyptos formed the chorus, and this in turn allows us to speculate that the focus of the second play was on the battle predicted in

Suppliants, or at least on its consequences. We know of a tradition that Danaos succeeded Pelasgos as king of Argos, which may have been a consequence of Pelasgos' death in battle. Late mythographers mention a siege of Argos that is lifted when Danaos agrees to the marriage of his daughters to the sons of Aigyptos. It seems entirely possible that *Aigyptioi* ended with the entrance of the would-be bridegrooms into Argos to claim their brides.

Two substantial fragments remain from *Danaids*, and although they do not tell us as much as we should like about the action of the play, both confirm as the likely subject the maidens' murder of their bridegrooms and its consequences. The first announces the singing of a traditional waking song for bridal couples on the morning after their marriage. The obvious (but by no means only) interpretation of these lines is that they refer with conscious or unconscious irony to the morning after the murder, when the bridegrooms are already locked in the sleep of death. The second, one of the loveliest fragments in all Greek poetry, is known to have been spoken by Aphrodite, the goddess of love, and presumably comes from the ending of the play:

> Holy heaven longs to pierce the land,
> and longing for marriage seizes earth. Rain,
> falling from the liquid sky, impregnates earth,
> and she, to benefit mankind, gives birth
> to grass for the herds and to grain, Demeter's gift
> of life. From the showers of this wedding flow
> the seasons when trees bear their flowers and fruits.
> Of all these things I also am the cause.
> (frag. 125 Mette)

Several accounts of the myth feature a trial, either of Danaos for ordering and abetting the murders or of Hypermestra for disobeying her father. Aphrodite's speech is thus commonly held to come from a trial scene, such as the one that brings

Aeschylus' *Oresteia* to a glorious close with the acquittal of Orestes and the reconciliation of his enemies. It might equally well come from a context in which the Danaids accept or celebrate a new marriage, also a feature of some versions of the myth. In any case, it seems to imply a resolution of the opposition of male and female and a triumphant vindication of eros, for so forceful a statement of love's cosmic power by so great a goddess surely prevailed in the end.[1]

Amymone, the satyr play that followed the three tragedies, enacted another story of a Danaid, making clear how closely knit the entire tetralogy must have been. The plot was based on an episode known to us from the mythographic tradition, in which Danaos sends his daughters, including Amymone, to search for water on the parched Argive plain. Amymone hurls a dart at a deer, striking a sleeping satyr instead, who promptly assaults her. Poseidon rescues the struggling maiden and then sleeps with her himself, revealing to her the unfailing springs at Lerna as a reward. The play will have offered a lighthearted variation on the tragedies' themes of sexual violence and fulfillment.

Reading Aeschylus' *Suppliants*

This brief review of the Danaid Tetralogy, limited as our information about it is, suggests some ways in which *Suppliants* hints at a resolution yet to come. To turn to the play, however, is to be assailed by unresolved conflicts and internal contradictions. We need look only at the daughters of Danaos themselves. They are "a flock of doves huddled / in fear of

---

[1] If this line of reasoning is correct, it excludes the version, best known from such Latin writers as Lucretius, Horace, and Ovid, in which the Danaids are punished in the underworld by having to carry water endlessly in leaky jars. For further discussion of the whole issue of reconstructing the lost plays, the interested reader is referred to the exhaustive study of A. F. Garvie, *Aeschylus' Supplices: Play and Trilogy* (Cambridge 1969).

hawks" (219–20), "a heifer trapped by wolves on a steep crag" (336), helpless women, powerless exiles cowering in fear; yet, they hold their suppliant wands as "weapons" (18), and by the middle of the play have forced a great king to his knees by threatening to use the "fine device" (453) of their women's sashes to hang themselves from the statues of the gods. They claim to be Argive, yet they seem deeply foreign; despite their prayers for peace and prosperity, they will bring conflict and death to the land that receives them. The Danaids' invocation of Io as mother, Zeus as father, brings all these conflicts into sharper focus. Io, like them, fled a pursuing male, yet when she finally stopped and received him, Zeus came not in violence but with the gentle and fulfilling touch and breath that brought their own line into being. This is the Io through whom they can claim refuge in Argos, the Zeus whom they invoke to protect them from men. (The opposing images of fertilizing breath and destructive stormwind run through the entire play.)

The list could easily be extended, but this much should make clear that the contradictions are not a matter of Aeschylean inadvertence; rather, they constitute the very fabric of the play. Scholars have long noted that what would seem to be the most basic question, "Why do the Danaids flee?" is given no straightforward answer, though of course many have tried to supply it. Do the women flee all men, or only their cousins? Do they reject submission, or male violence, or endogamy? It is not part of Aeschylus' design to make us decide; the issue is joined not so much at the level of the motivation of these particular characters as through divergent visions of the possible relations between men and women. The Danaids are caught in that stage of psychic development where marriage is by definition rape, and indeed the Aigyptioi, to judge by the herald they send to seize the women, are still rapists. In Zeus and King Pelasgos the Danaids see projections of the all-powerful male, but as substitute fathers, paternal guardians who will keep the violence of sexuality from them. Yet Zeus, by liberating Io at last with his gentle, lifegiving touch, and the king, by his concern for the safety of the entire community, show in different ways that men need not always be tyrants. Io shows the way to individuation and sexual maturity, to the fulfillment of motherhood, but only later will Hypermestra take the risk of sexual initiative and partnership.

Suppliants itself is inconclusive because the Danaids' rite of passage has only begun. Having forced Pelasgos' hand by the "device" (453) of threatening suicide at the altars of the gods, they pray to Zeus in the final lines for yet another "cunning device" (1092) to spare them the marriage they cannot accept. They are still praying for the wrong thing; they are not yet ready to make the passage to womanhood. Yet the Aigyptioi, from all we have seen and heard, are no more ready than they for marriage as real intimacy and mutual respect. They, too, in the person of Lynkeus at least, still must make the passage to a manhood not based solely on brute force. Despite the limitation of its characters and their vision, *Suppliants* does indeed suggest this movement still to come. In the dialectic of drama there are no simple truths, and in the poetry of their great odes the Chorus speaks better than it knows, pointing the way beyond all the contradictions and uncertainties to principles of reciprocity and love between the sexes that will come to fruition only later, and through yet more suffering. It is a theme that has not grown old.

A Note on the Text

To say that seven plays of the perhaps eighty-odd that Aeschylus composed have survived to this day is to put the matter too baldly. What survive are mutilated and error-ridden medieval copies of libretti for ancient performances that used, in addition to the spoken word, music, dance, gesture, and spectacle, about all of which we know very little. In the case of *Suppliants*, so much of which is devoted to choral song and dance, the loss of these components is especially to be regretted. Nevertheless, it seems clear that the verbal text was always paramount in Greek tragedy, with the other elements of stage performance designed to reinforce words spoken or sung. As a general rule, no significant action occurred (including entrances and exits) that was not marked in the text. For this reason, although the manuscripts contain no stage directions whatever, the text itself provides the information we need to supply them.

The manuscripts of *Suppliants* are riddled with corruptions and lacunae about whose extent and correction no two editors are in complete agreement. My translation corresponds to no single edition of the text, but I have benefited from consulting as many as I could lay my hands on. Along with every other student of this play, I owe a special debt of gratitude to the most recent editors, H. Friis Johansen and Edward W. Whittle, for their monumental and monumentally learned text and commentary (Copenhagen 1980), but the obligations of the translator are different from those of the scholarly editor. I have admitted many conjectures found only in their *apparatus criticus*, made the most of passages they consider corrupt beyond remedy, and in general have chosen not to emphasize the accidental inadequacies of our manuscripts. Instead, I have everywhere tried to give what I take to be the sense—at least the probable sense—of the original. But the reader who does not have access to Greek is hereby warned that what remains to us of Aeschylus' *Suppliants* is somewhat less complete and less certain than this translation suggests.

AESCHYLUS

The Suppliants

CHARACTERS

CHORUS of the daughters of Danaos

DANAOS

PELASGOS, King of Argos

HERALD of the sons of Aigyptos

HANDMAIDENS of the daughters of Danaos

Armed attendants

SCENE

A sacred grove outside the city of Argos
with an altar and images of several gods

PARODOS

The CHORUS *enters from the left, led by* DANAOS *and carrying branches wreathed in wool as tokens of supplication. They are followed by* HANDMAIDENS, *who seat themselves at one side of the orchestra, where they will remain in silence until the Exodos.*

CHORUS
Zeus,
      suppliant lord,
            turn your eyes
kindly toward us, travelers who raised sail
where the Nile slides through rippling sands
to the sea. We fled your land, the sun-stunned
pastures that stretch to Syria, not
because our townsmen banished us
for the stain of bloodshed; no, we flee
by choice, escaping men and chains we detest:
unholy marriage to Aigyptos' sons,
our kinsmen.   10
      Danaos, our father and the leader
of our rebellion, chose to play this pawn
as best among sorrows: so we skimmed
the salt rolling sea and reached harbor
here in Argos. We are Argive. We boast
birth from the fly-maddened heifer whose womb
the touch and breath of Zeus filled—Io.
What land would receive us more gently, armed

[5]

as we are only with suppliants' weapons,
these olive branches tufted with wool?

City, earth, trembling waters,   20
                    receive us!
Gods of sky and soil-dwelling spirits
whose home and honor lie deep,
                    receive us!
And you, Zeus Savior, third and last,
who guard the houses of the just,
                    receive
this suppliant troop of women, breathe
your mercy on us. Send sweet breezes.

The men, Aigyptos' brawling swarm,
                    destroy them!
Hurl their proud ship back onto the breakers
before one foot fouls this marsh.
                    Destroy them!
Rain-heavy gales pound, hurricanes   30
lash with lightning, thunder shake them,
sea swell crush and drag them to death.
                    Destroy them
before they mount (justice forbid!)
beds they have no right to, to rape their cousins.

During the following lyrics, the CHORUS *leaves its for-*
mation to dance.

        Calf,   *Strophe* 1
              child of Zeus
beyond the sea, I call you now
              to defend me,
child of our flower-browsing mother
        by the breath of Zeus,   40
        by the touch that ripened

at the hour appointed for Io
  to give you birth, rightly
    called Epaphos

  Child   *Antistrophe 1*
    of His Touch.
Now, in meadows where she once grazed,
    I remember
the mother of us all, her pain
    long gone that vouches   50
    for the story I tell.
I will show birth tokens, trusty signs
    to astonish Argos
      with truth in time.

If a reader of birdsongs comes near   *Strophe 2*
  he will hear
    in my cry
  the crying of Tereus' wife,
  hawk-harried nightingale,

who mourns for the green-leafed streams of *Antistrophe 2*
  home
    barred to her,   61
      and the child
    killed by her hand, her own hand
    in fierce unmothering rage.

I too love the dirge, and with wild song   *Strophe 3*
rip cheeks smooth-ripened in Nile sun,
    devour a heart
      unused to tears.
I pick grief's flowers and graze on buds of fear:
    are there no friends here   70
for my flight from the land broad as air, no kin
      to care for me?

[7]

Gods of my race, you birthgods, hear me!   *Antistrophe 3*
Look where justice lies: do not waste
    my youth on what
        must never be;
hate rude force and you are just to marriage.
    One altar shelters
even the warworn, one refuge for exiles:
        awe of the gods.   80

      Zeus's will be done—   *Strophe 4*
    though his desire is hard to track
and the paths of his mind stretch shadowed,
        tangled in thickets
    where I cannot trace or guess.

      What Zeus has decreed   *Antistrophe 4*
    by his nod stands fast, unshaken.
It blazes out everywhere, flares
        even in darkness
    the black flame of doom for men.   90

From their heaven-storming towers of hope   *Strophe 5*
    Zeus hurls men to ruin,
    yet his strength wears no armor,
        his force is all ease.
In the pure stillness where he thrones
    he wills thought to deed
        and the deed is done.

Let Zeus see men's insolence swell,   *Antistrophe 5*
    the stalk unfurling wild
    fresh tendrils to entwine us,   100
        flowering with wanton
wicked thoughts, frenzied with desire.
    Lust goads them to ruin:
        folly traps the fool.

[8]

Such suffering my keening tells, my shrieks   *Strophe 6*
        shrill with pity,
                heavy with tears.
    Ai   Ai   Ai
        Still living I sing
    my own dirge, my only prize.   110

                Hilly grazingland of healing Apis
                        hear me!
                Earth, you know my savage tongue.
                See, I tear my softspun Sidon veil
                        to tatters.

But if death stands aside and all is well,   *Antistrophe 6*
        these rites of death
                run stained toward god.
    Ah   Ah   Ah
        Wave on wave of grief,   120
    where are you carrying me?

                Hilly grazingland of healing Apis
                        hear me!
                Earth, you know my savage tongue.
                See, I tear my softspun Sidon veil
                        to tatters.

    Oars and a rope-rigged shelter   *Strophe 7*
            against the sea
                    sped us stormless,
    for the winds were kind. So far   130
            I find no fault,
                    and still I pray:
    all-seeing Father, grant us
                gracious issue.

                        [9]

Help us, the brood of a mother you hallowed,
escape the beds of men,
Oh   Oh   Oh
flee untamed, unwed!

Pure maiden daughter of Zeus,   *Antistrophe* 7
will as I will.   140
Guard of the gate
to the hallowed shrine, guard me
with all your strength.
Unbroken maid,
keep me unbroken, ward off
my pursuer.

Help us, the brood of a mother you hallowed,
escape the beds of men,
Oh   Oh   Oh
flee untamed, unwed!   150

If not, if sky gods spurn our sun-black tribe,   *Strophe* 8
we must turn to the god
who dwells in earth and welcomes wanderers,
Zeus of the dead,
we must turn these sacred fillets
to nooses.

Ah Zeus, for envy of Io
oh, how gods' vengeance
still stalks us.
I know the heaven-toppling anger   160
of your queen:
rough winds draw storms behind them.

Then my just reproaches will catch Zeus out,   *Antistrophe* 8
for he disowns the child

he himself once begot of the heifer,
     turning his glance
away from our prayers. No, hear us
     from on high!

     Ah Zeus, for envy of Io
          oh, how gods' vengeance   170
          still stalks us.
I know the heaven-toppling anger
     of your queen:
     rough winds draw storms behind them.

EPISODE I

The CHORUS *resumes its formation at one side of the orchestra.* DANAOS *stands near the altar.*

DANAOS
Be prudent, children! A prudent captain steered you
here, your trusty old father, and my advice
will serve on land, too. Write it in your hearts.
I see dust rising, voiceless herald of a marching
army; the whine of the axle trees spinning
in their sockets breaks the silence. Now   180
I can make out troops with bright shields
and bristling spears, horses and curved chariots.
Likely the country's leaders, learning from scouts
that we are here, have come to see for themselves.
But will they approach in peace or whetted
to savage anger? Better in any case, daughters,
to sit near the gods assembled on this hill.
An altar is stronger than any tower, a shield
no man can penetrate. Come quickly, holding
the white-crowned branches, emblems of Zeus who   190
    shows pity,
reverently in your left hands. You must answer the strangers
as strangers should, in piteous voices filled
with sorrow and need. Say plainly that this exile
is not stained by blood, but strike all boldness
from your words, and all immodesty
from your eyes; look downcast and gentle. Speak only

when spoken to, but then don't be slow in reply.
People here will be ready to take offence.
You are refugees and in need: remember
to be submissive. Proud speech is not for the weak.   200

CHORUS LEADER
Father, your prudent advice strengthens our prudence;
we have sealed it safe in memory. Now,
forefather Zeus, look down.

DANAOS
                                        May his eye
caress you with kindness. Come, no more delay.
Turn plan into deed.

                    The CHORUS *moves toward the altar.*

CHORUS LEADER
                            I will take my place at your side.
O Zeus! Have pity, do not let us die.

DANAOS
With his favor, everything ends well.
Now call upon this bird, sacred to Zeus.

CHORUS LEADER
We pray that the Sun's rays show us safety.

DANAOS
And holy Apollo, a god once exiled from heaven.   210

CHORUS LEADER
He knows our sorrow: may he show mercy to us mortals.

DANAOS
May he show ready mercy and defend us.

CHORUS LEADER
Which of these gods shall I call to witness next?

DANAOS
Here is a trident, emblem of the god . . .

CHORUS LEADER
                                who gave
us safe passage. May he keep us safe on land.

DANAOS
And this is Hermes, as the Greeks portray him.

CHORUS LEADER
Let him herald happy news of our freedom.

DANAOS
Honor the altar these lords all share, sheltered
in their purity like a flock of doves
huddled in fear of hawks that wear the same feathers   220
but defile the race, kinsmen and enemies at once.
Can bird devour bird and be pure? Can a man
marry against the will of the bride, against
her father's, and be pure? No, even in death
he would have to stand trial in Hades' house,
where they say a second Zeus judges
wrongdoing, against whose judgments there is no appeal.
Take care now to answer as I have instructed you.
Our cause will win.

> PELASGOS *and his attendants have entered the orchestra*
> *from the right, and now come to a halt before the* CHORUS.

PELASGOS
                        Foreigners, where are you from?
I greet a gathering splendid in robes and headdresses   230

[14]

such as no Argive wears, or any woman
of Greece. And your daring astounds me, seeing
you have come without criers to announce you
or patrons to prepare your way. Still, you have set
branches before the gods assembled here
in the manner of suppliants seeking refuge.
That is all a Greek can be sure of; for the rest,
though I might guess, your own voices will answer.

CHORUS LEADER
What you say about our appearance is true.
But how should I address you? Simply Sir,   240
or Reverend Priest of this shrine, or Royal Highness?

PELASGOS
Address me with trust and assurance: I am Pelasgos
son of Palaichthon, child of Earth, and I rule
this land. My people, called Pelasgoi after
their king, work the soil here and reap
its bounty. All the lands that stretch along
the sacred river Strymon toward sunset
belong to me. I rule the north beyond
what eye can see, past Mount Pindos to the land
of the wild Paionians and as far as Perrhaibia   250
and Dodona's ridge, where the oaks of Zeus
quiver out their oracles. Then the sea holds me back.
I rule whatever lies within these bounds.
Time out of mind the plain here has been named
for Apis, the healer, Apollo's son. From Naupaktos
across the gulf he came long ago
to prophesy and cure when bloodshed defiled
Earth's womb and made her spawn a deadly brood
of serpents to share our homes. Apis purged
the land of these monsters, cut out the sore   260
with perfect art, worked healing to save us,
and earned as wages a monument in grateful prayer.

You have heard my land and lineage; now tell me yours.
Be brief. We are not fond of idle talk.

CHORUS LEADER
Briefly, then, and clearly: we are Argive.
We claim to descend from the Cow blessed with child—
a proud claim, and our story will prove it true.

PELASGOS
Strangers, your tale beggars belief. How can
you be Argive? To me, you look like Libyan
women, not our native stock, or maybe   270
spawn of the fertile Nile. Cypriot craftsmen
stamp their coins with images like yours.
You might be nomads such as I have heard
saddle the ungainly camel and cavalcade
across some African landscape. If you had bows,
I'd take you for that tribe of husbandless hunters,
the flesh-eating Amazons. But tell me your story; I want
to learn how you claim the descent from an Argive line.

CHORUS LEADER
You know that here in Argos long ago
Io kept the keys of Hera's house?   280

PELASGOS
Indeed she did; everyone knows the story.

CHORUS LEADER
Do they also tell that Zeus made love to her?

PELASGOS
Yes; but could not hide his embraces from Hera.

CHORUS LEADER
So there was strife in heaven. How did it end?

PELASGOS
Our goddess transformed woman into cow.

CHORUS LEADER
And Zeus still pursued this horned creature?

PELASGOS
They say he took the form of a bull in rut.

CHORUS LEADER
How did his strong-willed queen answer that?

PELASGOS
She set a watchman, all eyes, upon the cow.

CHORUS LEADER
Who was this all-seeing herder of one heifer?   290

PELASGOS
Argos, son of Earth. Hermes killed him.

CHORUS LEADER
How else did Hera harass the poor cow?

PELASGOS
She sent a tormenting, cow-driving gadfly.

CHORUS LEADER
The Goad—that is the name Nile's people give him.

PELASGOS
And he drove Io from home on a zigzag trek . . .

CHORUS LEADER
Everything you say confirms my story.

[17]

PELASGOS
to Kanopos and as far as Memphis . . .

CHORUS LEADER
where the touch of Zeus's hand planted the seed.

PELASGOS
Who then claims to be the calf of Zeus's cow?

CHORUS LEADER
Epaphos, named for the prize Zeus seized.   300

PELASGOS
⟨And Epaphos' child?⟩

CHORUS LEADER
                    Is called Libye, because
she harvested the bounty of Earth's greatest river.

PELASGOS
What offshoot of hers do you still have to name?

CHORUS LEADER
Belos. He had two sons. One is my father here.

PELASGOS
This honored gentleman? Tell me his name.

CHORUS LEADER
Danaos. He has a brother with fifty sons.

PELASGOS
The brother's name? Surely you won't withhold that.

CHORUS LEADER
Aigyptos. Now you know your suppliants' lineage
from ancient times. We are Argives. You owe us protection.

PELASGOS
It seems you do have an ancient claim on Argos.   310
But what drove you to flee the house of your fathers?
What storms of fortune carried you away?

CHORUS LEADER
Lord of the Pelasgoi, trouble changes its colors
ceaselessly; misfortunes are not of a feather.
Who could have guessed that exile would cast us ashore
at Argos, fleeing the advances of our cousins
out of hatred for the marriage bed?

PELASGOS
What grace do your suppliant branches, fresh-cut
and wreathed in white, claim from this assembly of gods?

CHORUS LEADER
Not to be slaves to the sons of Aigyptos.   320

PELASGOS
Because you hate them? Or because it would be unlawful?

CHORUS LEADER
Would a woman scorn a master she loved?

PELASGOS
Yet it is through marriage that our strength increases.

CHORUS LEADER
Yes—and those in misery are left to their suffering.

PELASGOS
Then what am I, as a righteous man, to do?

CHORUS LEADER
The sons of Aigyptos will claim us. Don't hand us over!

PELASGOS
A heavy burden—it will mean a dangerous war.

CHORUS LEADER
Justice shields the man who fights for her.

PELASGOS
If she shared the struggle from the start.

CHORUS LEADER
Honor the helm of state wreathed by my branches.   330

PELASGOS
I shudder to see their shadow in this sacred place.

CHORUS LEADER
The wrath of Zeus Suppliant is a heavy burden.

> *In the following exchange, the* CHORUS *dances and sings;*
> PELASGOS *remains stationary.*

CHORUS
    Son of Palaichthon, hear me   *Strophe 1*
with a kind heart. Lord of the Pelasgoi,
    look on your suppliant, this exile,
a heifer trapped by wolves on a steep crag
      trusting still in her herdsman's strength,
        bleating for his help.

PELASGOS
I see them nodding, this company of gods assembled
in the shade of your fresh-cut branches. But may   340
the cause of these strangers, our kin, not bring us disaster,
not bring war without warning to a city caught
unprepared. Of such things we have no need.

[20]

CHORUS
    Themis, suppliant goddess,   *Antistrophe 1*
daughter of Zeus Allotter of Shares,
    see that our flight is free of disaster.
My lord, though old in wisdom, learn from youth:
    Revere your suppliant's righteous claim
        and win the gods' grace.

PELASGOS
This is not my hearth where you sit. If the whole   350
community risks infection, the people must find
a cure together. I can promise nothing
until I share the counsel of all my citizens.

CHORUS
You are the citizens, you are the state!   *Strophe 2*
    A king fears no judgment:
your nod is vote enough to rule
this altar, this common hearth;
    your throne and your sceptre
alone command in every need.
    Beware defilement!   360

PELASGOS
Defilement be with my enemies! But how
can I help you without terrible harm?
And if I should refuse to honor your prayers?
No one would call that gracious, or wise either.
I am at wit's end, fearing to act,
or not to act and take what chance may send.

CHORUS
Look up to him who watches from the heights,   *Antistrophe 2*
    patron of all who crouch
at neighbors' hearths, waiting in vain
for justice. The wrath of Zeus   370

Lord of Suppliants will not
be moved by the tears and groans of
        those it ravages.

PELASGOS

But if the sons of Aigyptos claim to rule
you as next of kin, in accord with the law
of your land, how can I oppose them?
You must show that those same laws
give them no power at all over your lives.

CHORUS

                May I never,   *Strophe 3*
            never fall into men's hands,   380
under men's power. My defense from this
marriage I loathe is escape; I will find
                my own cure
under the stars. Make Justice your ally, my lord.
            Choose to honor the gods!

PELASGOS

This is no easy judgment. Do not ask
me to judge. I have said it before:
although the power is mine, I will not act
without the people. I will not have them say,
"You honored strangers and destroyed your land."   390

CHORUS

                Zeus, our blood-kin,   *Antistrophe 3*
            your blood-kin, surveys all this,
a balance poised in his impartial hand.
The injustice of the wicked he heaps
                on one scale;
on the other, the holy deeds of the righteous.
            How can justice bring pain?

[22]

PELASGOS

We must search deep for a thought that can save us,
for an eye, clearsighted and unblurred,
to descend, like a diver combing the sea floor,   400
and surface again unharmed with an outcome
free of disaster for the state, and also
for myself. We don't want War to plunder here;
we don't want to invite Vengeance, destroyer
god who never sets his victims free
even in Hades, to settle on our house
for having surrendered you to foes as you sat
in the seats of the gods. We must search for a thought that
    can save us.

CHORUS

Think: *Strophe 4*
    think of justice, think of reverence.   410
        Be our patron,
        our protector.
    Do not betray us, exiles
driven far from home, pursued by violence
        that the gods despise.

You   *Antistrophe 4*
    hold all power here; will you watch me
        seized as booty
        from this altar,
    this seat of so many gods?   420
Know men's violence and its outrage; beware
        the anger to come!

    Can you bear to watch   *Strophe 5*
        suppliants dragged
from the gods' images by our headbands,
        like horses,
rough hands grasping at our finespun robes?

Know that your children   *Antistrophe 5*
        and your whole house,
whatever choice you make, will reap rewards   430
        or pay back
in kind. Think! The rule of Zeus is just.

PELASGOS

I have thought and thought, and am run aground
on necessity's steep shoals. Like a ship
with bolts fastened tight, gripped by ropes
and winches, I am being dragged to war
with these or those. Nowhere is there a harbor
free of pain. If a house is plundered, Zeus
the Enricher may send new wealth for old,
a shipload, more by far than what was lost.   440
If the tongue shoots its arrows amiss, its barbs
of bitter anger, speech may still heal speech.
But to keep from shedding kindred blood
we have mighty need of sacrifices.
Many victims must fall to many gods
to ward off ruin. Yes, I shrink from this struggle:
better to be ignorant of evil than an expert.
Yet may all be well, despite my judgment.

CHORUS LEADER

Hear the last of many righteous pleas.

PELASGOS

Speak! You may be certain I shall hear.   450

CHORUS LEADER

I have belts and sashes to tie my robes.

PELASGOS

Such things are suited to women. What of it?

[24]

CHORUS LEADER
Well, you see, they give me a fine device.

PELASGOS
What kind of talk is this? Come, speak plainly!

CHORUS LEADER
If you fail to make us a firm promise . . .

PELASGOS
How will your device of sashes serve?

CHORUS LEADER
To adorn these images with strange new offerings.

PELASGOS
This is a riddle. Tell me what you mean.

CHORUS LEADER
We mean to hang ourselves from these gods—right now!

PELASGOS
The words I hear are whipstrokes to my heart.   460

CHORUS LEADER
Then you understand. I have opened your eyes and you see.

PELASGOS
Yes—see troubles to wrestle wherever I turn,
a flood of evils churning like a river
that sweeps me toward a bottomless sea of destruction,
treacherous to cross, and with no haven from harm.
If I do not settle your claim in full, you threaten
defilement that cannot be overtopped; but if
I take my stand before the walls and fight
Aigyptos' sons, the issue will be bought

[25]

at bitter cost indeed: men's blood staining   470
the plain for women's sake. Yet the wrath of Zeus
Lord of Suppliants commands our awe and reverence.
His fear is highest.

(to DANAOS)

You, the girls' old father,
take these boughs and go to other altars
of our gods. Let all the citizens see a sign
that you come as suppliants, and not take me
to task, quick as they are to blame their leaders.
The sight may even stir pity and dispose
some to despise the violence of the men.
The people will favor you in this extremity,   480
for everyone grants good will to the weak.

DANAOS

It is no small thing to gain a righteous patron,
and one so kind. But send an escort to guide me
safely to the altars that stand before your temples,
homes of the gods who guard this state. I look strange;
the race Nile breeds is unlike Inachos' tribe.
Alone, my boldness might give birth to fear,
and men have killed friends through ignorance before.

PELASGOS

(to a group of his attendants)

March with him, men; the stranger, our guest, is right.
Lead him to the city's altars and the seats of the gods.   490
And don't prattle with passers-by. You are simply
escorting this sailor as a suppliant to the gods' hearths.

Exit DANAOS *right, attended and carrying a bundle of branches.*

CHORUS LEADER
He has your orders and is on his way.
But what of me? How can I hope to be bold?

PELASGOS
Leave your branches here as a sign of your troubles.

CHORUS LEADER
I leave them. I am obedient to your word.

PELASGOS
Now move along toward this open precinct.

CHORUS LEADER
How can a space that is open to all protect me?

PELASGOS
We'll not give you up for winged monsters to seize.

CHORUS LEADER
What of those more hateful, more vicious than vipers?   500

PELASGOS
My words have been fair. Let yours not be ill-omened.

CHORUS LEADER
Do you wonder that fear drives out reason?

PELASGOS
But a woman's fears are always excessive.

CHORUS LEADER
Then cheer my spirit with your words and deeds.

PELASGOS

Your father will not abandon you for long,
but first I am going to call the Argives to assembly
to win their good will for you, and I must teach
your father how to address them. You wait
here and pray to Argos' gods to grant
what you desire. I go to arrange the rest: 510
May Persuasion attend me, and Luck be our ally!

PELASGOS *and his retinue exit right.*

STASIMON I

The CHORUS *dances.*

CHORUS

Lord of lords, blest   *Strophe 1*
beyond all blessing, blissful Zeus,
        yours is the power
in perfect fulfillment.
        Hear me! If you hate
        the violence of men,
    keep your kin safe from outrage,
    break calamity's black oar
        in the dark sea-swell.   520

        Look with kindness   *Antistrophe 1*
on women of a glorious line,
        renew the gentle
tale of love for Io,
        whom your touch once made
        mother of us all.
Remember your long wooing!
We claim you as our father
        and this land as home.

        My mother's ancient track   *Strophe 2*
        I retraced to this field   531
        where under watchful eyes
    she nibbled flowers, then fled,

[29]

stung to madness by her fly,
trading one tribe for the next
on her mindless trek, until
    she swam the wind-tossed strait
and her fate gave the cleft between continents
    its name: Cow-ford.

    She lunged across Asia,   *Antistrophe 2*
    through sheep-grazing Phrygia,   541
    past the towns of Mysia,
up the Lydian valleys
to Pamphilia's mountaintops,
and onward to Cilicia.
Over rivers whose waters
    always flow she fled,
through Aphrodite's deep dark soil that yields rich
    scythings of grain.

The winged cowherd goaded her on.   *Strophe 3*
    Frantic with pain   551
she reached Zeus's fruitful meadows
snow-fed by sacred Nile
no illness touches, but whirlwinds lash.
Io was crazed with shame, inflamed,
    possessed by Hera's goad.

Natives trembled with pale terror   *Antistrophe 3*
    at what they saw,
uncanny hybrid woman-cow,
    a marvel, a monster!   560
Who was it then healed Io, released
the careweary wanderer from
    the torture of the goad?

    Zeus Who Rules All Time   *Strophe 4*
    caressed her with might,

with tender breath
freed Io from pain.
She poured out her sorrow
in tears of shame.
Truly the cargo she now took on   570
was Zeus's, his the perfect
child she bore,

whose time was happy   *Antistrophe 4*
and long. So the Earth
cries aloud, 'This,
this is Zeus's child,
son of him who gives life!
Who else could heal
the plagues Hera's cunning hate contrived?'
Zeus's this work: and our race   580
his child's line.

What god have I clearer   *Strophe 5*
claim in justice
to summon for his deeds
than the Father
who planted my seed with his own hand,
great architect of our race,
allhealer, old in wisdom,
Zeus of fair breezes?

He sits below the throne   *Antistrophe 5*
of no other,   591
to no power pays homage,
does no one's work
but his own. His deeds are accomplished
with the whisper of a word
that brings to birth whatever
his fertile mind wills.

[31]

EPISODE 2

Enter DANAOS *from the right.*

DANAOS
Children, take heart! The people have voted
to support us with the full force of law.

CHORUS LEADER
Dear old man, best herald of my hopes!   600
Tell us: What was the final decision, how
did the majority rule in the show of hands?

DANAOS
It was a sight to make my old heart young
again—the air bristling with hands raised
unstintingly, without a moment's doubt,
as the Argives decreed that *we may settle
here in freedom, safe from seizure and assured
of protection. No one, native or foreign,
shall drag us off, but if enemies try force,
the price to any citizen who refuses aid*   610
is loss of rights and exile. King Pelasgos
won our case with a warning not to fatten
the wrath of Zeus Lord of Suppliants.
Twofold defilement, he said, arising alike
from claims of natives and strangers, would wander the
       state,
grazing unchecked, insatiable for suffering.

The people of Argos heard and stretched their hands
high even before the vote was called.
Skillful turns of speech persuaded them,
but Zeus put his seal on the outcome, too. 620

DANAOS *moves to the altar and stands looking to the left*
during the following song.

CHORUS
Come, let us pray for Argos,
returning good for good.
May Zeus Lord of Guests and Strangers
guide blessings from the mouths of guests
faultless to their goal.

STASIMON 2

The CHORUS *dances.*

Zeus-born gods,   *Strophe 1*
hear us now as we pour
libations of blessing on Argive kin:
Let lewd Ares, who harvests men
    where others sowed the seed,   630
        never raise his cry,
        desolate music
        fit for no dance,
above the fire-toppled towers of Pelasgos' town.

For they pitied us,
cast a vote in all kindness,
honored Zeus's suppliants,
this unenvied herd.

They did not   *Antistrophe 1*
    spurn a woman's battle   640
to vote with men. They watched the avenging
eye of Zeus, exactor of debts,
    the gaze that can not be
        outfought. What house
        would ask for Vengeance
        to perch heavy,
defiling the rafters like some bird of ill omen?

Argos honors kin,
suppliants of Zeus the Pure,
and so her spotless altars   650
will win the gods' grace.

Let prayers eager to bring honor   *Strophe 2*
fly up from my veil-shadowed lips:
        that no plague empty
        the town of men, no strife
drench this soil with its children's blood;

        that the flower of youth
            grow ungathered,
        that Ares Manslayer,
        who beds Aphrodite,   660
            not mow down their blooms.

And let the altars where elders   *Antistrophe 2*
assemble blaze at their tending.
            The state is governed
            well when Zeus gets his due,
the strong guest god whose law guides straight.

        May this land bear leaders
            always, we pray,
        and may the Farshooter
        Artemis watch over   670
            each mother's birthpangs.

Let no killing quarrel rip   *Strophe 3*
            the state to tatters,
        rousing Ares to arms,
father of tears, who hates the dance,
            who shuns the lute,
arming brother against brother.

[35]

May the hateful swarms of sickness
  settle far away.
May Apollo Wolfgod
  be kind to the young.

Zeus grant earth to swell with fruits   *Antistrophe 3*
  in perfect ripeness
season upon season.
Let the cattle that graze this plain
  bear countless calves.
Let all blessings flow from the gods.

Let harpers raise their hymns of praise
  at every altar.
Let songs that love the lyre   690
  pour out from pure lips.

  The people rule this city: *Strophe 4*
may they guard their rights without flinching
  and govern with forethought
    for the common good.
And let them grant fair terms to strangers,
  not arm Ares for battle:
    do justice, not harm!

  Gods dwell here and keep this land: *Antistrophe 4*
worship them in the ancestral way,   700
  cutting the laurel and
    slaughtering cattle
as your fathers ordained. For Justice
  has made honoring parents
    her third commandment.

EPISODE 3

DANAOS
For these prudent prayers, my children, I have
nothing but praise. And now you must listen bravely
to your father's unwelcome, unexpected news.
From this refuge for suppliants, my lookout, I spot
their ship. There is no mistaking those sails, the sides   710
shielded with hides, the eyes of its prow scanning
a course through the waves, eager, all too eager
to do the tiller's bidding, but no friend to us.
Now I see sailors, black limbs glistening against
white tunics; now other vessels—a whole fleet
carrying troops to do their masters' bidding.
The lead ship has furled sail close to shore
and is rowing in at full stroke.
                              Calm
and prudence are needed now, and you must never
neglect the gods that shelter here. I shall go   720
rouse advocates to defend you, for a herald
or a whole delegation may try to seize you,
drag you away as booty. No! They shall never
touch you. No need to tremble on that account.
But if our help is slow, you can do no better
than remember this refuge, all your strength.
Courage! In time, on the destined day, every
man who scorns the gods will surely pay.

In the following exchange, the CHORUS *dances and sings,*
DANAOS *and the* CHORUS LEADER *remain stationary.*

CHORUS LEADER

Father, I am frightened. Their ships have wings.
   Only moments divide us now.   730

CHORUS

              I tremble with terror!   *Strophe 1*
Has all my running really come to this?
         I die from fear, father.

DANAOS

Courage, children! The Argives' vote was final
   and they will fight for you, I know.

CHORUS LEADER

Aigyptos' tribe is accursed, wild with lust,
   battle starved. You know that, too.

CHORUS

         In dark-cheeked, strong-hulled   *Antistrophe 1*
              ships
they sailed against us, a great black army.
         Their anger hits its mark!   740

DANAOS

Yes, but row on row of men, limbs toughened
   under the sun, will meet their charge.

CHORUS LEADER

Do not desert me, I beg you! A woman alone
   is nothing. There is no strength in her.

CHORUS

         But the men are   *Strophe 2*
full of blood lust, treacherous,
         impure of heart,
ravens eager to defile an altar.

[38]

DANAOS

We are the winners, children, if they add
    the gods' hatred to our own.   750

CHORUS LEADER

No awe of tridents or the gods' other emblems
    will keep their hands from me, father.

CHORUS

    So arrogant,   *Antistrophe 2*
  swollen with unholy rage,
    the shameless dogs
will hardly hear the gods commanding "No"!

DANAOS

Wolves are stronger than dogs, the proverb says.
    Papyrus is no match for wheat.

CHORUS LEADER

This is a raging, lustful beast, an unholy
    terror. We must protect ourselves!   760

DANAOS

A fleet needs time to get under way and time
to put in at port. Even when a ship
rides at anchor and the hawsers are secured on shore,
the wise steersman is still wary, moored
off a harborless coast, with the sun sinking
into the sea. Night brings pangs like childbirth
to the sailor shepherding his flock of ships. And no troops
will disembark until their vessel is secure
in her moorings. You are frightened, I know; but keep
your wits about you and don't neglect the gods.   770
⟨I go to make all ready for you, once⟩
I have persuaded our allies to help. Old
as I am, they will find my wits and words still young.

      Exit DANAOS *right.*

STASIMON 3

The CHORUS *dances.*

O hills and pastureland   *Strophe 1*
worthy of so much awe,
        what must we suffer?
Is there in all Apis' country
no dark hollow to hide me?
O to fly up, away, black smoke
        among Zeus's clouds,   780
        or wingless dust
vanishing into sheer nothing!

No escape from this fate!   *Antistrophe 1*
My heart shudders darkly.
        I am trapped, trembling
in the net father's watching set.
Better death in a noose's
embrace than let the man I loathe
        graze my skin with his
        greedy fingers.   790
Sooner Lord Hades possess me!

Can I find some high throne   *Strophe 2*
where dripping clouds congeal to snow?
        Or must a sheer brooding crag,
        goat-shunning,
        vulture-haunted,
        aloof,

[40]

watch me fall before brute force makes a marriage
    to break my heart?

    Then let dogs feast, let birds   *Antistrophe 2*
tear my flesh, no matter. To die   801
    is to stand clear of evils
       that fatten
       on groans and tears.
     I choose
death, not marriage. How can I cut a path to
    deliverance?

    Burst heavenward, my cry: *Strophe 3*
let my lament find fulfillment
     from the gods,   810
     find some release!
Father, look with eyes of justice
flashing out hatred of force: honor
    your suppliants, almighty
      Landruler Zeus!

    The spawn of Aigyptos   *Antistrophe 3*
pursue me with ruthless male pride,
      swaggering,
       howling their lust,
storming this refuge to take me   820
by force. But your hand holds the balance;
   men achieve nothing except
     you will it so.

EPISODE 4

The HERALD *of the sons of Aigyptos enters left with armed followers.*

CHORUS
Aaah!
He has crawled ashore, this sailor,
and comes to seize me!
before you take me, you die!

HERALD
Move down to the ships, now,
move along!

CHORUS
I'll scream!   830
I see the suffering
start, the violence against us.
Aiai!
Run! Make for safety,
for our refuge!
They're savage-minded,
their lust unbearable
on land, on sea.
Lord of the land,
defend us now!   840

HERALD
Get going!
Move along,

[42]

along to the ships.
What? You won't?
You won't? I'll tear
out your hair, pluck
you clean, brand you.
I'll chop heads from
blood-gushing stumps!
Get going, damn you.   850
To the ships!
Move!

CHORUS
            The salt waves   *Strophe 1*
      should have swirled over you,
the current engulfed your rugged ships—
      and your masters' brutal pride.

HERALD
I'll drag you
bleeding, throw you
into the boat.
Stop screaming.   860
Are you mad
to die? Hey!
Away from the altar!
To the ships!
You have no rights,
no honor.
You think I'll
feel reverence?

CHORUS
            I pray you   *Antistrophe 1*
      will never see again   870
the flood that brings forth cattle, that warms
      and ripens blood to bear life.

[43]

HERALD

. . . .

To the ship now,
to the ship quick!
Like it or not,
I'll drag you off
by force, right now,
by force.

. . . .

CHORUS

Ai!   Ai!   Ai!   *Strophe 2*

      May you die helpless   880
in the sea's cold embrace,
stiff gales drive you headlong
      across her salt plain,
smash you against the sandbar they call
      Sarpedon's barrow.

HERALD

I order you on board, quick! Our prows
point seaward. No more delay: I'll not be
ashamed to drag you off by the hair.

CHORUS

Ah!   Ah!   Ah!   *Antistrophe 2*

      Outrage! Mad dogs howl   890
lecherous at my heels.
May great Nile see you rut
      and turn you away
with your ignorant pride and stupid
      arrogant power.

HERALD

Howl, shriek, cry to your gods: still
you'll not jump ship on Aigyptos' sons!
Fiercer screams! New wails to match new woes.

CHORUS

    Father, your help fails me,   *Strophe 3*
    the altar tricks me.   900
Like a spider he traps me,
        drags me seaward
step by step. A dream?
      A black nightmare!

Oh!   Oh!   Oh!
    Mother Earth,
Mother, save me!
    Turn away
his frightful shout!
    Father Zeus,   910
o son of Earth!

HERALD

I am not afraid of the local gods.
They did not rear me, they will not feed my old age.

CHORUS

    A huge two-legged snake   *Antistrophe 3*
    darts close, eagerly
lunges at his helpless prey—
        hideous viper,
    he grasps my foot in
        horrible jaws!

Oh!   Oh!   Oh!   920
    Mother Earth,
Mother, save me!
    Turn away
his frightful shout!
    Father Zeus,
o son of Earth!

HERALD

If you don't give in and move along to the ship,
I'll have no pity, I'll tear your clothes to shreds!

CHORUS LEADER

Rulers of this land, they are breaking me!

HERALD

Since you won't listen to me, it seems   930
I shall have to drag you off by the hair.

CHORUS LEADER

Lord Pelasgos! We are done for! The pain!

HERALD

If it's a lord you want, you'll soon see lords
enough—sons of Aigyptos! You won't lack masters.

> *As the* HERALD *and his men continue to pull the*
> CHORUS *from around the altar,* PELASGOS *enters*
> *left with a band of soldiers. At his first words,*
> *the struggle ceases.*

PELASGOS

You there! What are you doing? How dare you treat
The land of the Pelasgoi with such contempt?
Or did you imagine only women live here?
Barbarians who play these insolent games
with Greeks soon find they have badly missed the mark.

HERALD

Are my actions unjust? What gives offense?   940

PELASGOS

First, you don't know how strangers should act.

[46]

HERALD
How so? I am just recovering lost property.

PELASGOS
What patron's support have you called on here in Argos?

HERALD
The greatest there is: Hermes, patron of searchers.

PELASGOS
You claim a god's support for sacrilege?

HERALD
The gods I honor live beside the Nile.

PELASGOS
And the gods of Argos are nothing. Is that what you mean?

HERALD
I mean to take these girls, unless you steal them.

PELASGOS
Lay one hand on them and you'll howl with pain!

HERALD
This is how you befriend a foreign guest?   950

PELASGOS
Steal from the gods and you're neither friend nor guest.

HERALD
Very well. I'll report this to Aigyptos' sons.

PELASGOS
What do I care? You don't graze my meadows.

HERALD

Before I go—a herald's first duty
is precision. What shall I tell my lords?
Who robs them of their cousins? Ares will
not call witnesses in this dispute,
nor settle it by levying a fine. No, first
many will fall, many cast off their lives.

PELASGOS

Why tell my name? You and your whole crew   960
will learn it soon enough. But you shall have
the women only if they wish it so,
only if honest persuasion wins their consent.
Our people will never give them up to force;
Argos voted as one man, and bolted it
clear through, like a hull, to hold it fast.
This is not something scratched on tablets or sealed
in scrolls; it is the plain speech of a free tongue.
Now get out of my sight and be quick about it.

HERALD

So, we stand on the brink of a dangerous war,   970
it seems. Victory and power to the men!

PELASGOS

You'll find men here, too—who drink a stronger
brew than barley-beer.

    The HERALD *and his followers exit left.* PELASGOS *turns
to the* CHORUS.

                 Take heart,
all of you! Go with your own attendants
to the safety of our city, impregnable
behind strong walls and towers designed
with deep cunning. You will find there

many houses belonging to the people,
and my house, too, laid out with a generous hand.
You are welcome to share lodgings with others,   980
or to live apart in separate dwellings,
if that should please you more. The choice is yours.
I am your patron and sponsor, along with all
the citizens whose vote brought this about. What
higher authority can you be expecting?

CHORUS LEADER
May the good you have done,
most godlike of the Pelasgoi,
blossom with good in return.
But we ask one more favor:
send us boldhearted Danaos,   990
our father, to guide our thoughts.
He will know where we should dwell.
Although you now welcome us kindly,
people are quick to fault foreigners.
May it all end for the best.
May our reputation stay fair
and without reproach in Argos.

PELASGOS *and his followers exit right. The* CHORUS
LEADER *now addresses the* HANDMAIDENS, *who have
been seated at one side of the orchestra since the beginning
of the play.*

Handmaidens, each of you stand
beside the mistress whose dowry
Danaos made you, to serve her.   1000

As the HANDMAIDENS *move to the side of their mis-
tresses,* DANAOS *enters right, accompanied by an armed
escort.*

[49]

DANAOS

Children, we owe prayers to the people of Argos,
burnt offerings and outpourings of wine, as if
to the gods of Olympos, for they are truly saviors.
What happened here they heard with loving care
for you, their kin, but hatred for your cousins.
And to me they have assigned this company
of spearmen, to do me honor and protect me
against plots to strike me down, making
my death an everliving burden on the land.
In return for such favors, let thanks fill   1010
the sails of your hearts, and add one prudent thought
to the many your father has written in your minds:
Time will be our judge, for we are strangers
here. Slander stands on every tongue,
ready to defile us with a hasty word. Do not
bring me shame! You are at the age that
turns men's eyes. Ripe fruit is hardest to guard,
for men will covet and plunder, even birds
and beasts will ravage it. And why not?
Aphrodite herself hawks this fruit   1020
of her fairest season bursting with sweet nectar,
and passers-by, struck by desire for lush
maiden beauty, shoot volleys of enchanting
glances. Do not fall to what we have struggled
to flee, plowing the furrowed seas. No shame
for us, no pleasure for our enemies!
Live where you like: both Pelasgos and the city
offer quarters free of cost. That much
is easy. Only hold firm to your father's command:
Honor modesty more than life itself!   1030

CHORUS LEADER

The gods grant all else, but as for my ripe
fruit, father, take heart. Unless the gods
lay strange new plans, I'll not stray from my track.

[50]

EXODOS

The CHORUS *sings and dances the first strophic pair, the* HANDMAIDENS *perform the second.*

CHORUS
Glory and honor to the gods,   *Strophe 1*
    blessèd lords of Argos
who hold the town in their hands, and who dwell
    along Erasinos
ageless, everflowing. Attendants,
    mark my song: I shower praise
        on Pelasgos' state   1040
and my hymns no longer honor
    Nile spilling seaward,

but sing the rivers that rise here,   *Antistrophe 1*
    gentle, shining waters
that pour through the land to sweeten the soil
    and make it rich with young.
Pure maiden Artemis, turn your eyes
    toward our troop in pity,
        spare us marriage rites
compelled by force. I'd seek that prize   1050
    on the shores of Styx.

HANDMAIDENS
        We are your friends, but our flock   *Strophe 2*
        will not scorn Aphrodite

[51]

the Wily, honored for her awesome power,
who stands with Hera nearest Zeus's throne.
Her darling daughters are at her side,
   Desire and Persuasion,
who cast inescapable spells.
  Harmony, too, has her part
    in lovers' whispers   1060
  down well-worn paths of loving.

  I fear for the fugitives: *Antistrophe 2*
  stormwinds are rising, cruel griefs
and blood-smeared war threaten. Why else the smooth
crossing, swift pursuit? If fate has ordained
a thing, it will be. The mind of Zeus
    is trackless, unbounded.
Marriage has come to so many
  women now and in time past;
    I too add a prayer   1070
  for willing consummation.

*The third strophic pair is divided between the two groups
facing each other on opposite sides of the orchestra.*

CHORUS
  Great Zeus, guard us from   *Strophe 3*
marriage with Aigyptos' sons!

HANDMAIDENS
And yet that would be best.

CHORUS
Your charms will not charm *me*.

HANDMAIDENS
You know nothing of the future.

[52]

CHORUS
    No. Can my eyes pierce   *Antistrophe 3*
to the depths of Zeus's mind?

HANDMAIDENS
Then moderate your prayer.

CHORUS
What must the limit be?   1080

HANDMAIDENS
Don't ask the gods for too much grace.

CHORUS
    Lord Zeus, spare us   *Strophe 4*
bitter marriage to mates we despise.
    You who delivered
Io from pain with hands of healing,
    making gentle your might,
give women power and victory!

    I am content   *Antistrophe 4*
if my portion of evil is mixed
    with a share of good,   1090
if Justice renders judgment for me.
    Lord, grant me some cunning
device to win my deliverance!

    DANAOS *and his attendants exit right in solemn proces-*
sion, followed by the CHORUS *and* HANDMAIDENS.

NOTES

1 **suppliant lord**: Zeus, the most powerful of the Olympian gods, was regarded by the Greeks from Homer onwards as the protector of wanderers and all who seek refuge.

23 **Zeus Savior, third and last**: an allusion to the custom of pouring three libations after a meal, of which the last was offered to Zeus as protector of home and family.

45f. **Child of His Touch**: Aeschylus plays on the name Epaphos and the common noun *ephapsis*, "touch."

58 **Tereus' wife**: usually called Prokne, she punished her husband for his rape of her sister Philomela by murdering their own son Itys. Tereus' wife was transformed into a nightingale, Tereus into a hawk (elsewhere, a hoopoe).

111 **hilly grazingland of healing Apis**: the Greek words *Apian bounin* refer to the land of Argos, for which Apia was an alternate name (cf. the reference at 255 to Apis, the heroic healer), but also glance at the maidens' claim to be Argive by oblique allusion to Io (in the phonic similarity of *bounis* and *bous*, "cow") and to Apis, an Egyptian calf-god identified with the Greek Epaphos.

139 **Pure maiden daughter of Zeus**: Artemis, virgin goddess of the hunt, a resolute protector of virginity.

154 **Zeus of the dead**: Hades, lord of the underworld; cf. 224ff.

160f.   **the heaven-toppling anger of your queen**: the jealous wrath of Hera; see 279ff.

208   **this bird, sacred to Zeus**: must be the eagle, a regular companion of Zeus, but in the following line the Chorus identifies it with the sun, apparently alluding to the Egyptian solar hawk of Amun-Re.

210   **once exiled from heaven**: Apollo killed the Cyclopes because they made the thunderbolt with which Zeus killed his son, Asklepios. For this, Zeus banished him from Olympus for a year, during which he served the Thessalian king Admetos as a shepherd.

214   **a trident**: symbol of Poseidon.

216   **Hermes, as the Greeks portray him**: apparently another instance of "translating" between a Greek representation and the corresponding Egyptian one. This Hermes presumably appears as an heroic human figure; the Egyptian messenger-god Thoth was represented as ibis- or ape-headed. Alternatively, Danaos may make euphemistic reference to a phallic image of the god such as could be seen everywhere in the Athens of Aeschylus' day.

234   **patrons to prepare your way**: *proxenoi* were individuals who announced the arrival and represented the interests of foreigners; the Danaids will appeal to Pelasgos himself to become their patron (411), and Danaos will call him patron when he has accepted their suit (482).

243   **Palaichthon**: the name means simply Ancient Land; through him, Pelasgos claims what the Greeks referred to as autochthony, the racial purity of a line sprung directly from Earth, and thus not subject to the uncertainties of migrations, invasion, or even sexual generation.

246   **All the lands**: the kingdom grandly claimed by Pelasgos encompasses essentially all of mainland Greece, from Thrace in the northeast to Epirus in the west.

291 **Argos**: by most accounts had a hundred eyes and enormous strength; to kill him, Hermes had first to lull him to sleep eye by eye with his music.

300 **named for the prize Zeus seized**: a second etymology of the name Epaphos (the first is alluded to again in 298, **the touch of Zeus's hand**.) The play on words here is more complex; Epaphos is said to be named after *rhusia*, meaning something taken or seized as compensation; the missing verbal connection is the verb of seizing, *ephapto*; the conceptual connection is that Epaphos' name, by alluding to the divine seizing of Io, declares him to be its true compensation.

301 A line has dropped out; the bracketed words supply the needed question. **Libye** is evidently associated here with the fertile region of the Nile, not the area encompassed by modern Libya. (The Greeks commonly used the name to refer to Africa as a whole.)

344 **Themis**: as a common noun, "custom" or "law"; Hesiod makes the deity Zeus's bride, by whom she bears Justice and Good Government, among other offspring; here, she is his daughter or simply his agent, but in any case personifies the force that binds societies together and regulates conduct.

350 **my hearth**: the hearth and its fire were the sacred center of domestic life, and every settlement also had a public hearth that in some way both symbolized and guaranteed communal life. The hearth of a home would be the appropriate place to supplicate a powerful individual. (We know that a contemporary of Aeschylus, the great statesman and general Themistocles, became a suppliant at the hearth of Admetos, king of the Molossians, when he was ostracized from Athens.) Pelasgos distinguishes such private supplication from the demand that the Danaids are making of the whole Argive people. The Danaids reply by assimilating the altar to the public hearth and the King's will to that of the whole state (354–60).

[57]

375 **as next of kin:** Pelasgos appears to know of an Egyptian law that gives the Danaids' cousins some claim to take them in marriage. There is no evidence that such a law existed, but the Athenian audience might well be aware that intermarriage was customary within the pharaoh's family, and they would think also of the Athenian law conferring the right to marry an heiress upon her father's next of kin, though this applied only after the father's death. The Chorus evade the legal question, but the Herald of the Aigyptioi raises it again at 942, and it may have played a role in the following play, *Aigyptioi*.

486 **Inachos' tribe:** the people of Argos, after one of the two chief rivers that water the Argive plain.

527 **Remember your long wooing:** translates the Greek phrase *genou polumnestor*, which simply means "be much-remembering"; but the adjective also suggests *mnester*, "suitor," especially in a line addressed to *ephaptor Ious*, "the toucher of Io."

539 **Cow-ford:** a literal translation of *Bosphorus*, as the strait that divides Europe from Asia Minor is still known. The word does not occur in Aeschylus' text; I have taken the liberty of making his allusion explicit.

548 **Aphrodite's deep dark soil:** i.e., Phoenicia, famous for the cult of Astarte, whom the Greeks assimilated to Aphrodite.

629 **lewd Ares:** he is the type of the adulterer from the *Odyssey* onward (cf. 660), but the epithet here primarily refers to his "promiscuous" conduct in war; as in matters sexual, so in battle he is always taking what does not belong to him.

669f. **Farshooter Artemis:** like her brother Apollo, Artemis is an archer. The Greeks associated her equally with the protection of virginity (see on 139) and the easing of childbirth.

680 **Apollo Wolfgod**: perhaps an allusion to the Argive sanctuary of Apollo Lykeios, the chief glory of Argos, according to the geographer Pausanias, and supposedly founded by Danaos. As Wolfgod, Apollo is chiefly a figure of destruction, but he may here be invoked as undoer of harm, or simply propitiated so he will not cause harm.

705 **third commandment**: the first two are contained in 696–703, fair treatment for strangers and honor for the gods. The gods might be expected to come first in such a triad, but the Chorus has every reason to emphasize hospitality to foreigners.

723 **drag you away as booty**: the Greek phrase, *rhusion ephaptores*, carries an ironic overtone of Epaphos, the product of Zeus's seizing of Io; see on 300.

761ff. Danaos' description of the difficulties of landing an army, a somewhat awkward way of calming his daughters' fears, takes on a (no doubt unconscious) double meaning when we realize that images of anchoring and harboring can be Greek metaphors for sexual union. Danaos' words seem to suggest a slow, careful preparation for a nocturnal climax— that ironically will bring the pangs of childbirth upon the males.

771 Once again I have supplied in brackets a line that has dropped out of our manuscript tradition.

774 **O hills and pastureland**: the Greek says *io ga bouni*, which is close in sound to "Io, Earth, Cow" (cf. on 111).

871 **the flood that brings forth cattle**: i.e., the Nile.

873 The beginning and end of this speech are mutilated beyond plausible restoration.

885 **Sarpedon's barrow**: a headland on the Cilician coast opposite Cyprus; Sarpedon is the Lycian king known from

the *Iliad*. The Chorus at this point imagines a disastrous return voyage of its enemy to Egypt.

942 **recovering lost property**: see on 375.

943 **What patron's support**: see on 234.

1037 **Erasinos**: one of the two principal rivers that flow near Argos (the other, the Inachos, is mentioned at 486). It is contrasted at the end of the strophe by the Nile, and at the end of the antistrophe by the Styx, chief river of Hades.

1052 The final chorus must be divided between two parties, but there is no clear indication in the text as to how, and three possible solutions have vigorous scholarly adherents: (1) the Danaids divide themselves into two half-choruses, (2) the Danaids are answered by the Argive bodyguard that has returned with Danaos, (3) the Danaids are answered by their Handmaidens. I have chosen the last alternative as most consistent with the indications of the text and most dramatically appropriate, but the matter is impossible to resolve with certainty.

The Lockert Library of Poetry in Translation

George Seferis: Collected Poems (1924–1955), translated, edited, and introduced by Edmund Keeley and Philip Sherrard

Collected Poems of Lucio Piccolo, translated and edited by Brian Swann and Ruth Feldman

C. P. Cavafy: Collected Poems, translated by Edmund Keeley and Philip Sherrard and edited by George Savadis

Benny Anderson: Selected Poems, translated by Alexander Taylor

Selected Poetry of Andrea Zanzotto, translated and edited by Ruth Feldman and Brian Swann

Poems of René Char, translated by Mary Ann Caws and Jonathan Griffin

Selected Poems of Tudor Arghezi, translated and edited by Michael Impey and Brian Swann

"The Survivor" and Other Poems by Tadeusz Różewicz, translated and introduced by Magnus J. Krynski and Robert A. Maguire

"Harsh World" and Other Poems by Ángel González, translated by Donald D. Walsh

Ritsos in Partheses, translations and introduction by Edmund Keeley

Salamander: Selected Poems of Robert Marteau, translated by Anne Winters

Angelos Sikelianos: Selected Poems, translated and introduced by Edmund Keeley and Philip Sherrard

Dante's "Rime," translated by Patrick S. Diehl

Selected Later Poems of Marie Luise Kaschnitz, translated by Lisel Mueller

Osip Mandelstram's "Stone," translated and introduced by Robert Tracy